MW01068549

Career As A Navy SEAL

What They Do, How to Become One, and

What the Future Holds!

Brian Rogers

KidLit-O Books

www.kidlito.com

Table of Contents

About KidCaps

KidLit-O is an imprint of BookCaps™ that is just for kids! Each month BookCaps will be releasing several books in this exciting imprint. Visit are website or like us on Facebook to see more!

Two Navy SEALs carrying out their mission[1]

Introduction

Burt Thompson and his platoon were nervous. They were sitting down on plastic chairs bolted to the inside hull of a C-130 Hercules aircraft. All sixteen of them were packed into the cargo bay, forming a platoon of Navy SEAL Team 1. Once the large door of the C-130 lowered, they would jump out of the back of the cargo bay and parachute down into enemy territory. It was to be their first mission as a team.

It was dark inside the aircraft, and the soldiers had been ordered to limit radio chatter to only the most necessary communication. Burt wanted to see how his men were feeling. After all, for a couple of them, this would be their first real taste of action. The Air Force crew of the C-130 was flying high enough to avoid detection by passive enemy radar below and was also limiting their talk over the radio. It wasn't unusual for SEALs to get rides from the Air Force to their missions, and Burt found that he respected his fellow soldiers no matter what the color of their uniform was. But personally, Burt was glad to be a SEAL.

Tonight, his platoon would be performing a HALO (High Altitude-Low Opening) jump. That meant that plane they would be jumping from had to stay at a high altitude so that the enemy's surface-to-air missiles couldn't reach it. After the soldiers jumped, they would have to wait a few extra seconds before opening their parachutes close to the ground. They did this to avoid being detected by enemy radar and to minimize the time that that they would be easy targets for enemy soldiers on the ground below. A HALO jump like this is one of the most dangerous things that a soldier could do- and Burt was so excited that he could barely wait.

Half an hour earlier, the men had spent some time breathing pure oxygen in preparation for the jump. The pure oxygen removed any excess nitrogen from their bloodstreams, which helped them to avoid getting severe cramps during the HALO jump they were about to make. Burt reached up his hand, almost without thinking, to make sure that his oxygen mask was still firmly attached to his face and that the tube leading to the tank was connected. He would need that extra oxygen during the jump. At such high altitudes, there wasn't much oxygen in the atmosphere, and aside from the pain, Burt might pass out without enough air and be unable to pull open his parachute when the time came.

Burt looked at his fellow SEALs sitting on the other side of the cargo bay and could tell that they, like him, were feeling the beginnings of an adrenaline rush. They were all experiencing that same strange mixture of emotions: nerves, excitement, and impatience to get moving. After months of training, this was the first real mission for some of them, and first mission for the team as a whole. They had all performed HALO jumps during training, but there was something different about doing one when you were flying over enemy territory.

The Air Force Loadmaster of the C-130 walked down the middle of the cargo bay waving his hands- the signal that the time to jump had arrived. Burt and his men all stood up began to inch towards the end of the gangway. As the Loadmaster pushed the controls, the large cargo bay door began to lower, and soon a space large enough to drive a Humvee through had opened up for Burt and his men. The SEAL Platoon Leader raised and lowered his arm, the signal for the men to start jumping. Without a word, they all started moving down the tailgate to the cavernous opening. The wind roared as Burt moved closer, step by step to the end of the tailgate. After three pairs of soldiers had jumped, it was his turn. Without thinking twice, Burt let his training take over and jumped out into the black night.

The rush was incredible. The sound of the air passing by his mask was overwhelming and deafening. He used his compass to veer off to the south as agreed upon to avoid colliding in the dark with the other SEAL who had jumped with him. After counting to twenty-five, Burt pulled the rope on his pack and deployed his parachute. He looked around him but couldn't see any of his fellow soldiers, although he knew that they were there. Based on the altitude of the plane and the time he waited to deploy his parachute, Burt knew that he was going to experience about two minutes of controlled falling. He grabbed the handles above his head and began to steer himself towards the predetermined meeting point. He couldn't see the landing zone yet, but he knew that the illuminated compass he carried would keep him moving in the right direction.

An Air Force Combat Controller had already landed on the ground and had marked out a protected landing area. Once Burt got close enough he should be able to identify it. Time moved quickly, and within a few minutes Burt had landed safely on the ground, gathered up his parachute and stowed it into a bag, and pulled out his weapon. He had been given the order to secure the perimeter while the rest of the platoon landed, and that is exactly what he did. Within a few minutes, all sixteen men were on the ground, and together with the Combat Controller they moved closer to their target.

The first phase of the mission had been accomplished- and now the dangerous part was about to begin.

***

Have you ever wanted to be a part of something truly special? Have you ever wanted to play for the winning team and to know that your life has a real purpose? Have you ever wanted to use your energies and abilities to help other people, especially those who can't always help themselves? Then perhaps the life of a Navy SEAL is for you!

In this handbook, we will be learning all about taking up a career as a Navy SEAL. What would you like to learn about this interesting job? We will be looking at seven different areas, and by the time you are done reading this handbook you will know a whole lot more about being a Navy SEAL.

First, we will talk about what a Navy SEAL is. Did you know that SEAL is an acronym that actually stands for something? Do you know how long Navy SEALs have been operating? You will find out in the first section. In the second section, we will find out what the training is like to become a Navy SEAL. You will see how all interested recruits must pass through 61 weeks of intense training to qualify, and that these recruits are pushed to their physical, mental, and emotional limits. The training is hard, but for those who make it a life of adventure and respected service awaits them!

Then we will answer the question: Is being a Navy SEAL an easy job? You can decide the answer for yourself as you learn about what is needed to be a SEAL from one day to the next, and what some past missions that SEALs have been sent on were. After that, the fourth section will give us an exciting look into the average day of a Navy SEAL. Do you know how long their missions last, and what kinds of places they serve in?

Then, in the fifth section, we will see what the hardest part of being a Navy SEAL is. While many people think about the training as the most difficult part, in reality the day to day life of a Navy SEAL can be pretty hard too. We will look at three of the things that make being a SEAL tough.

The sixth section will consider what the future holds for Navy SEALs. In ten years, when you are old enough to become a SEAL, what can you expect the job to be like? What kinds of factors will change and which ones will be the same? We will see how new technology and the changing face of warfare are making Special Forces like the SEALs more important and valuable than ever before. Finally, in the seventh section you will get to learn what steps you can take right now to get ready for an exciting job as a Navy SEAL. Even though you have to be at least 18 to apply for SEAL training, there are several things that you can do in the meantime to help with your success. This section will show you what those steps are.

Becoming a Navy SEAL means having an important job with a rich heritage- and while not everyone is cut out to be a Navy SEAL, you can be sure that those who make it through the training become an important part of America's military. Are you ready to learn more? Then let's get started!

Chapter 1: What Is a Navy SEAL?

Navy SEALs wearing diving gear, coming out of the ocean, ready for action[2]

---

[2] Image source: http://commons.wikimedia.org/wiki/File:SEALS_wearing_diving_gear.JPG

Navy SEALs are part of the military's Special Forces, along with Army Rangers, Air Force Combat Controllers, and Marine Force Recon groups. All soldiers who make up Special Forces groups are highly trained to be able to carry out any mission that they are given.

The Navy SEALs got their start way back during World War Two. The United States government knew that the fighting in Europe and in the Pacific at the time would be difficult, and thought that highly trained soldiers could do a lot to guarantee the safety of the invasion forces that would arrive later. Certain Navy sailors were chosen to participate in a new program called the Navy Scouts and Raiders. These sailors were trained to launch little boats off of submarines and to prepare the beaches for invasions by large numbers of troops. They sabotaged enemy equipment, marked landing areas for boats, and assisted in different ways during the actual invasions. The Navy Scouts and Raiders were able to complete several successful missions in Africa and Europe during World War Two.

In the meantime, other groups of elite sailors were being trained in similar areas- these groups were called Navy Combat Demolition Units. They specialized in using explosives to clear the way for boats, men, and vehicles when invading a foreign country. Navy Combat Demolition Units helped to make the Allied landings at Omaha and Utah Beaches successful, as well as the various landings in the Pacific Island Campaign against Japan.

These two groups gave soldiers valuable experience in something called "unconventional warfare". Have you ever heard that phrase before? "Unconventional warfare" means fighting wars using new and different tactics. By the early 1960s, President John F. Kennedy could see that the future of war was changing. Instead of lines of soldiers marching side by side and conquering one city after another, the United States military could expect to see more of what it had seen during the Korean War- guerrilla warfare. Instead of clearly marked battle lines, guerrilla warfare would involve sneak attacks, ambushes, and sabotage. The United States had to adapt to this new way of fighting against their enemies. In fact, events in Southeast Asia convinced President Kennedy that there would soon be another war using guerrilla tactics.

On May 25, 1961, during the same speech where he promised to put a man on the moon, President Kennedy announced that over $100 million would be spent to improve the US special operations forces. He wanted to improve America's use of unconventional warfare and to train American soldiers in guerrilla tactics. In January of 1962, the first two Navy SEAL teams were formed.

Do you know what "SEAL" stands for? It is an acronym, which means that each letter actually stands for a word. SEAL stands for "SEa, Land, and Air". The idea was to train soldiers who could be used anywhere, anytime, for any mission. Whether they had to jump out of a plane, dive off of a boat, or sneak across enemy lines, these soldiers would get the job done.

The SEALs' first deployments were against Communist Cuba. They were sent just in case that country decided to start a war with the US or with any friends of the US. The SEALs took pictures and gathered information for a possible US invasion.

Later on, SEALs were sent to Vietnam both before and during the Vietnam War. They tried to interrupt the transportation of North Vietnamese goods through the river systems, and they fought hand to hand with North Vietnamese soldiers.

The North Vietnamese began to call Navy SEALs "the men with the green faces" because of the camouflage paint that the SEALs wore.

After the Vietnam War, Navy SEALs were among the most highly-decorated soldiers both for their acts of bravery and success on the battlefield. They had earned an excellent reputation, and future generations of SEALs would try and keep that excellent reputation even under the most difficult of circumstances. The Navy SEALs continued to participate in many military missions through the years, including the Gulf War in 1990-1991 and in the Afghanistan and Iraq Wars starting in 2001. The SEALs worked to provide information for invading forces, helped to search for and destroy large supplies of weapons, and fought alongside their fellow soldiers from other divisions of the military.

Do you have a better idea of what a Navy SEAL does now? They are expected to do some of the most impossible jobs, and they are often the first ones that go into a battle zone to make the area safer for everyone else. Their excellent training lets them do what few other soldiers can and to always have success in their mission- no matter what that mission may be.

Chapter 2: What Is the Training Like to Become a Navy SEAL?

Sailors training to be Navy SEALs must often stay for a long periods of time in freezing cold water[3]

_____

[3]   Image   source:
http://commons.wikimedia.org/wiki/File:%27Hell_week%27_--
_August_2004.jpg

As we have seen, being a Navy SEAL means being able to handle just about any mission that you might be sent on. Navy SEALs are expected to jump out of planes from high altitudes at night, to use explosives to sabotage enemy equipment, and to come ashore without alerting enemy guards. But as is the case with any job, no one is born with these skills- they must be learned. Before being named a Navy SEAL, sailors must successfully complete an average of 61 weeks of specialized training, after which they will receive another 18 months of special education before being sent out on their first mission with their assigned team. How is the training organized and who can apply?

Right now, only male Navy sailors between the ages of 18-28 can apply for SEAL training, and they must be United States citizens. All throughout the process, the different instructors will be focusing on what kind of person each recruit is. Although each recruit has to have a certain level of physical fitness, the instructors will mainly be looking at the attitude of each recruit. They want to know if each potential SEAL can take orders, can work as part of a team, and can make good decisions even when under extreme pressure or near exhaustion. One instructor puts it this way: "We are looking for the humble professional."

Training to become a Navy SEAL begins with a special eight week training course to prepare recruits for the BUD/s training (which we will talk about in one moment). This eight week course focuses on getting recruits physically ready for the challenges that await them. The recruits run, swim, and do lots of push-ups and pull-ups. To graduate from the BUD/s course, recruits must be able to do at least 50 sit-ups in two minutes, 50 push-ups in two minutes, 10 pull ups in a row, swim 500 yards in under 12:30, and run 1.5 miles in under 10:30. However, those are the *minimum* numbers, and much more is expected from a SEAL. This eight week preparation course gets the recruits physically ready for BUD/s training.

The next step towards becoming a SEAL is a course called BUD/s, which stands for Basic Underwater Demolition/SEAL training. This course lasts 24 weeks and pushes many sailors to their physical and emotional limits- only one out of every three recruits finishes the first phase of BUD/s training. What makes BUD/s so difficult?

The training begins with a three-week period of orientation and then has three different phases of training. The orientation is pretty easy, just showing the recruits around the naval base in Coronado, California, where they will be staying for the course, as well as preparing them for the next three phases. Phase One focuses on Physical Conditioning, Phase Two focuses on

Combat Diving, and Phase Three focuses on Land Warfare. What can you expect to experience after the three week orientation? Let's look at each of the phases of BUD/s training to get an idea of what the recruits go through.

Phase One- Physical Conditioning: The first three weeks of Phase One are called Basic Conditioning. The recruits must spend lots of time getting their bodies ready for week 4, called Hell Week. During Basic Conditioning, recruits swim five days a week, run Mondays, Wednesdays, and Fridays, and train with weights on Tuesdays and Thursdays.

During Hell Week (Week 4 of Phase One) recruits experience twenty hours-plus of extreme physical activity each day. They run over 200 miles, carry boats high over their heads, run obstacle courses with real guns being fired near them, carry out "evolutions" (exercises) in the freezing cold water, and carry large logs from one place to another. During Hell Week, recruits might only sleep a total of four or five hours.

The point of this extreme physical activity is to see which recruits can stay focused even during difficult situations and which recruits refuse to give up no matter how challenging the situation. The instructors also want to show the recruits who don't quit how much their bodies are truly capable of.

After Hell Week ends, the recruits who haven't rung a special bell (telling everyone that they quit) will spend the final three weeks of Phase One reading and making maps of bodies of water, including measuring the depth, shorelines, and ocean floor.

Phase Two- Combat Diving: Phase Two of BUD/s training focusing on preparing recruits for swimming and diving during missions. They train for long-distance underwater swimming using SCUBA gear as well as basic underwater medicine. The goal is to teach future SEALs how to get from their "launch point" (an offshore boat or submarine) to their "mission objective" (their target somewhere on shore). Recruits even learn about the science (the physics) behind diving.

Phase Three- Land Warfare: During Phase Three, recruits learn more about carrying out their missions when on land. They learn to handle various types of weapons, how to set and detonate explosives, how to improve their aim when using different kinds of guns, and how to use a rope to drop out of a hovering helicopter when arriving at the battlefield. They also learn how to navigate over land and how to work together with a small unit to accomplish the missions assigned to them.

All during BUD/s school, the minimum times for different exercises (running, swimming, completing an obstacle course) are lowered, which means that the recruits are expected to perform better and better each time that they participate. The final three and a half weeks of Phase Three are spent on San Clemente Island (an island owned by the Navy off the coast of California) where all of their BUD/s training is put to use.

All recruits who successfully pass the difficult 24-week BUD/s training are approved to move on to Parachute Jump School. Although it only lasts for three weeks, this school is intense and teaches recruits how to jump out of airplanes at different altitudes and at different times of day (including pitch-black nighttime jumps).

Up to this point, recruits have survived the 8-week prep school, the 24-week BUD/s course, and the three week Parachute Jump School. They have spent the better part of almost six months exclusively focused on becoming

SEALs. They have learned how to handle themselves under extreme pressure while on the Sea, in the Air, and on Land. They are in the best shape of their lives and have shown that they do not give up easily, even when being pushed to their limits. So what happens to these recruits now?

They are invited to spend the next 26 weeks at SQT (SEAL Qualification Training). During the next four and a half months, the recruits who have shown exceptional qualities will receive the training that takes them from being just hopeful recruits to being truly qualified Navy SEALs. SQT takes everything that the recruit has learned up to that point and teaches them how to use it in the field on real life missions. They are flown to Alaska to learn how to survive freezing cold temperatures, they practice fighting hand-to-hand in cramped buildings, and they learn to use shoulder-mounted rocket launchers to destroy targets.

SQT also includes a special training given to all Special Forces- a program called SERE (Survival, Evasion, Resistance, and Escape). At a special location in Maine, SEALs are taught how to Survive and Evade capture in case their mission goes wrong or they are separated from the rest of their unit and from outside help. Then, in case they are captured, they are taught Resistance and Escape, which focuses on how to remain strong and loyal even when being mistreated by the enemy.

At the end of the 26-week period of SQT, all who complete the program are given the Navy SEAL trident for their uniforms, officially making them Navy SEALs.

The trident given to SEALs at graduation[4]

Once they have completed SQT, most new Navy SEALs must complete about one more years' worth of training before they get their first mission, and some will require up to 18 months' worth of further training. What will they be learning for these 12-18 months? Although each soldier will have been given the overall skills to be a SEAL, now they must be trained for their specific role in the team. Some will be trained as medics, others as snipers, and all will learn how to work as part of a unit, whether launching from

[4] Image source: http://commons.wikimedia.org/wiki/File:US_Navy_SEALs_insignia.png

submarines deep underwater or when being picked up by a helicopter using a specially-designed extraction ring.

Each phase of the training is as realistic as possible. For example, combat training includes pop-up targets, smoke, explosions, and gunfire. The SEALs are exposed to the confusing conditions of real battle zones as soon as possible in order to get them used to it. The SEALs try their best to improve each time, no matter how hard the drill is. They follow the motto "The more you sweat in peacetime the less you bleed in war", which means that the more they train and the better they get at their jobs, the more successful they will be when carrying out their missions in real life.

After the advanced training, SEALs will be placed into one of the eight SEAL teams operating around the world. Each SEAL team is sent out on missions ("deployments") which can last anywhere from 6 to 8 months.

Altogether, Navy SEALs will have received almost three years' worth of intensive training before being sent out on their first mission. Each phase of the training will have pushed them to new limits, but those who didn't give up will have learned how much they were actually capable of doing.

Chapter 3: Is Being a Navy SEAL An Easy Job?

As we have seen, the training to become a Navy SEAL is incredibly challenging. Between 80% and 90% of the recruits who start the training quit before they are finished. But once the recruit has finished training, has been officially named a SEAL, has received his advanced training, and has been assigned to a team, does that mean that his life is a vacation now and that he can sit back and take it easy? Not at all. Have a look at another Navy SEAL motto that shows how they think about their life:

<u>"The only easy day was yesterday."</u>

That phrase gets to the heart of how SEALs view their training, their job, and themselves. They didn't choose this job because it was easy- they chose it because they wanted to work hard. All throughout their training, they never stopped to look for the easy way out. They want to work, and they expect each day to be harder than the last, they expect each day to have a more challenging mission and to give them more difficult circumstances. Navy SEALs are called when the stakes are high and when the task is nearly impossible. SEALs are the ones who are called in to do what no one else can.

In order to truly appreciate what being a Navy SEAL is like, let's look at two recent missions Navy SEALs were sent on and see what the Navy SEALs involved were expected to do.

MISSION 1: Rescue hostages from Somali pirates: On April 8, 2009, four Somali pirates pulled up alongside a large American container ship named the *Maersk Alabama*. The ship had a crew of 20 and was carrying relief supplies for the people of Kenya. Despite the efforts of the crew of the *Alabama* to avoid being boarded by the pirates, the pirates were able to hook a ladder onto the larger ship and climb aboard. The crew tried to fight them off, but they were no match for the large guns carried by the pirates.

The pirates soon realized that the boat was too big for them to sail by themselves, so they decided to take the captain of the ship, Captain Richard Phillips, hostage with them on one of the ship's lifeboats. They would call some fellow pirates and wait for more people to arrive to help them take the ship and its cargo home to Somalia. They would also take the captain with them and demand millions of dollars for his release.

The American destroyer *USS Bainbridge* was nearby and was sent to help resolve the situation, arriving the next day, April 9. Soon after, a frigate ship named the *USS Halyburton* arrived on the scene. The pirates were getting scared, and were starting to reconsider their plan. Even though they had friends on the way, they were secretly counting on the Navy treating them fairly.

Meanwhile, in the White House, newly-elected US President Barack Obama had authorized the use of deadly force against the pirates if Captain Phillips' life was in danger. The Captain had to be rescued, but the rescue had to be carried out in such a way that the pirates didn't get the chance to hurt him before then. Who could handle such a difficult mission?

There was no question in anyone's mind: they had to send in the Navy SEALs.

A special team of Navy SEALs (formerly called Team Six, but now known as United States Naval Special Warfare Development Group [NSWDG], or DEVGRU) was sent out from their base in Virginia directly to the coast of Somalia. They performed a HALO jump at night into the ocean and then boarded the *Halyburton* at 2:30AM on April 11 before being transferred on a small boat to the *Bainbridge*- they had brought their own guns with them.

The next day, one of the four pirates essentially turned himself over to the Americans, asking for medical attention. He was taken on board the *Bainbridge* while the other three stayed on the lifeboat with Captain Phillips. After four days of being a hostage, Captain Phillips couldn't take it anymore and tried to escape the night of April 12, but the pirates stopped him. One of them, while doing so, fired his rifle into the ocean. It was clear that things were getting dangerous.

The Navy SEALs lay down on the back deck of the *Bainbridge* (which was now towing the lifeboat) and got ready to end the situation. As soon as all three pirates showed their faces at the same time, the SEALs used their sniper rifles to simultaneously shoot each of them in the head with one bullet each. In the blink of an eye, Captain Philips was rescued, and the crisis ended- thanks to the precision shooting and timing of the Navy SEALs.

The lifeboat where Captain Phillips was held hostage, tied to the back of the *Bainbridge*[5]

[5] Image source: http://commons.wikimedia.org/wiki/File:USS_Bainbridge_tows_the_lifeboat_of_the_Maersk_Alabama.jpg

MISSION 2: Find and capture/kill Osama bin Laden: The terrorist attacks of September 11, 2001 were a dark time for the American people. Through much investigation, it was learned that the mastermind of the attacks was a Saudi Arabian terrorist named Osama bin Laden. For many years, he managed to escape capture by the United States government even though there were many people working hard to try and find him.

In 2011, however, the many hours of searching finally paid off. In April, it was learned that bin Laden was hiding in a large compound in Pakistan. A replica of the compound was built, and Navy SEALs from DEVGRU began to train for a special mission using this replica. Finally, on May 2, 2011, at 1 AM, the SEALS arrived at the compound in Pakistan, brought in by two stealth helicopters. Half of them rappelled down from a helicopter into the compound, but the helicopter began to have problems and had to make an emergency landing (it was later blown up by the SEALs to protect any enemies from using it again). The other half of the SEALs climbed over the high walls using ropes and climbing equipment.

The team moved inside the compound, using explosives to open the doors from one room to the next. They found bin Laden hiding in a bedroom and took him down. Then they radioed the president directly and said "E.K.I.A.", which was code for "Enemy Killed In Action". President Obama, who was watching the situation as it unfolded, said, "We got him".

The Navy Seals had been able to carry out their mission in just 38 minutes- the objective had been reached, and zero Americans died during the mission.

Can you imagine what it would have been like to have been asked to participate in either of those two missions? Both of them seemed almost impossible, but thanks to the intense training and abilities of the SEALs involved, both missions were able to overcome any potential problems and to carry out their missions successfully.

Chapter 4: What Is An Average Day Like For a Navy SEAL?

An average day for a Navy SEAL depends on where he is assigned. If he is back in the United States on his base, his days will be spent training and continuing his education. He will also make sure to keep himself in excellent shape, which means days filled with running, swimming, and weight training.

But the moment that a SEAL team receives a mission, all of their energies focus on carrying out that assignment. They will research, plan out possible problems and decide what solutions to use, and practice specific skills for each mission. For example, the SEALs who invaded Osama bin Laden's compound in Pakistan had to practice close combat skills, wall climbing, using small explosives, precision shooting, and handling captives. They also had to perform a quick yet detailed search of the compound to locate any possible information about future terrorists or terrorist attacks.

Once they are deployed, SEALs spend long days marching through difficult terrain, gathering information, keeping guard, and fighting alongside fellow soldiers. Sometimes the missions are short and specific (like in the case of rescuing Captain Phillips) but other times the missions might involve supporting another SEAL group or even training and helping soldiers from a friendly country- missions that may last weeks or even months. In times like those, the day to day life of a SEAL is quite different.

SEALs travel the world and work in all kinds of environments. They parachute from planes, launch underwater from submarines, and drop down using ropes hanging from helicopters. It is hard to predict what they will be doing tomorrow, but they can always be sure that it will be exciting.

SEALs drive Light Strike Vehicles (like the one above) in their missions[6]

---

[6] Image source: http://en.wikipedia.org/wiki/Light_Strike_Vehicle

Chapter 5: What Is the Hardest Part of Being a Navy SEAL?

After the information that you have seen so far, are you interested in becoming a Navy SEAL? Do you think that you have the strength, the humility, and the perseverance to join this elite group of warriors? We have already seen that to become a SEAL, recruits must endure and do well during years of intense training. They must be able to run and swim long distances, carry heavy bags of equipment when marching and jumping out of planes, and must think clearly and work as part of a team even during the heat of battle or after working long hours without sleep.

But aside from the training, what is the hardest part of being a Navy SEAL? If this is a career that you are seriously considering, then it is good to be aware of both the good and the bad.

One of the hardest parts of any job in the military is that fact that, as a soldier, you must be ready to take the life of another human being. Think about that for a second- are you capable of killing another person? In a battle, where things happen fast, SEALs are taught to rely on their training- which involves the use of deadly force to protect themselves and others. While there is no doubt that there are bad people in the world and that some of them will not stop doing bad things as long as they are alive, not everyone is capable of being the person who actually pulls the trigger.

Another difficult part of being a soldier has to do with the time spent away from their home. Unlike most jobs, where workers can go home each night to be with their families, many soldiers (and especially Navy SEALs) must spend weeks and months away from the people they love-including friends and family. SEALs have to spend lots of time in far off places, and during missions they often don't even have access to a telephone or computer to talk with loved ones. Can you imagine going weeks or even months without speaking to your friends and family? Some fathers even miss seeing their kids grow up.

Some people also have a tough time with the secrecy that must be maintained as a Navy SEAL. SEALs know things that other people can't know- if they spoke about the things that they know (like who they work with, where they have worked, or what tools and weapons the military has) then the enemies of the United

States might use this information to hurt innocent Americans or US soldiers. As a result, the governing belief of each Navy SEAL is summed up on their official website:

> "I humbly serve as a guardian to my fellow Americans always ready to defend those who are unable to defend themselves. I do not advertise the nature of my work, nor seek recognition for my actions."[7]

Navy Seals do not talk about where they have been, what they have done, or who was there. Even if they participate in something incredible, like the rescue of Captain Phillips, they do not announce it to the world or demand special recognition. They simply stay silent and are happy to have been able to do their job.

---

[7] Quotation source: http://www.sealswcc.com/navy-seals-ethos.aspx#.UaOQUUA-bL0

Could you keep a secret like Navy SEALs do? Could you participate in exciting missions and then not tell anyone back home about what you did, even if they ask you about it? Not everyone has that kind of discipline, but we can be sure that the world is a safer place for all the soldiers (including Navy SEALs) who don't reveal classified (secret) information.

Chapter 6: What Does the Future Hold for Navy SEALs?

In recent years, because of some high-profile and public missions, Navy SEALs have started to get a lot of attention. Of course, it was not attention that they themselves looked for- in the majority of cases no one even knows the names of the SEALs involved in those missions. Even so, all this attention has got people talking about how effective SEAL teams are, and what their future might be. What do you think: will Navy SEALs still be working in ten years? Will the way that they carry out their missions be any different from how they do it today?

The answers might surprise you.

In early 2012, two hostages (including an American aid worker) were rescued by about two dozen Navy Seals. No SEALs were hurt during the rescue operation, and both of the hostages survived the attack. The world was impressed, and some experts have started to say that Special Forces are the future of warfare. What do they think that Special Forces will be more important in the future?

Instead of moving large armies into place and fighting long battles that last months and years, Special Forces (like SEALs) can move in quickly and calm situations down. Imagine if Navy SEALs had been around to stop Adolf Hitler once things started going bad. Many experts feel that militaries in the future will focus more on controlled missions and less on large-scale invasions- like the ones the United States oversaw in Iraq and in Afghanistan.

Also, there is plenty of new technology being developed that will make SEALs even more effective in the future. Among them is a flying car (pictured below)

A flying car that is being developed by the Defense Advanced Research Projects Agency (DARPA)[8]

New technologies (like flying cars) will allow Special Forces to be able to surprise enemy

[8]   Image   source:
http://en.wikipedia.org/wiki/File:Transformer_AVX.JPG

targets and avoid being destroyed by them. Working together with personnel on military bases, SEALs and other special forces will become even more useful in the future, especially as America's enemies stop being defined as entire nations and armies and are more closely identified as smaller groups and even as individuals.

In the next ten years, Navy SEALs will be more needed and more important than ever. They will be able to get into places where large armies never could and they will be able to carry out precise missions thanks to their training and cooperation.

Chapter 7: How Can You Get Ready Now to Become a Navy SEAL?

Are you 18 years old yet? If not, then you still have to wait a while before you can apply for SEAL training. But even if you still have a few years to go, there are a lot of things that you can do right now to get ready. What are some of the things to do?

1) Learn how to work as part of a team. Navy SEALs are not lone wolves- they work as part of a team. They know how to take orders, and they know how to cooperate. Behind every Navy

SEAL out on a mission, there are about 20 other people working behind the scenes to make sure the men out in the field have the right equipment, information, and transportation to get the job done and come back safely. If those SEALs didn't know how to work as part of a team, the job would never get done.

Start now cooperating with other people. On group projects at school, learn how to make sure that everyone does their part and be sure to do your part, as well. Consider joining an organized sport, like football, basketball, or baseball, and learn to listen to your coach and to work side by side with the other players.

2) **Develop the skills of a leader.** Navy SEALs need to be able to command other people when the situation calls for it. But being a good leader doesn't mean bossing other people around- it means giving each person the best job for their unique talents. It means keeping good

communication and making everyone feel like they are contributing to the success of the group.

Learn how to be a leader now, maybe by running for office at your school, by getting a job and being promoted to a supervisor, or by being the voice of reason with your friends. Don't try to make other people think like you, but help everyone around you to do their best, no matter what the situation may be. After all, that's what a good leader should do.

3) Study hard at school and don't get into trouble. Although being a SEAL has a lot to do with being in good physical shape, it also has a lot to do with being smart. A Navy SEAL needs to learn how to read maps, operate high-tech equipment, and communicate well. Studying hard at school can help you to develop the reading and math skills that you will need as a SEAL and can teach you how to express yourself clearly, even in moments of intense pressure.

Also, people who have problems with drugs or with the police can't be SEALs. So keep yourself out of trouble. Learning to obey the rules now can help make you a good SEAL later on, and it may even save your life someday when you are out on a mission.

4) Get in great shape now. Becoming a Navy SEAL will mean passing lots of physical tests. You will be expected to perform at a very high physical level as long as you are a SEAL. So when should you start getting ready to pass the basic requirements? Right now!

If you were to wait until enlisting with the Navy to train, you wouldn't have enough time to get ready. You would be far behind the rest of the recruits, which means that you might not make it through the first eight week preparatory session.

So start now. What kinds of goals should you aim for? As we saw earlier, to graduate from the BUD/s course, recruits must be able to do at least 50 sit-ups in two minutes, 50 push-ups in two minutes, 10 pull ups with no time limit, swim 500 yards in under 12:30, and run 1.5 miles in under 10:30. Those are the *minimum* numbers, which means that you should try to do even better. Talk to a doctor before you start exercising, because they can give you some good advice and make sure that you don't get hurt during your training.

Along with the above steps, you can also begin to educate yourself and learn as much as you can about being a Navy SEAL. Try to read books and do some online research to find out exactly what a Navy SEAL does. Find out as much as you can, and start learning that same types of things that SEALs learn, so that by the time you go through the training you are already familiar.

Speaking with someone who has been a SEAL, or who with someone who knows a SEAL, can be a wealth of valuable information for you, and your local Navy recruiting station can answer a lot of your questions. You can also go to the SEALs section of the official Navy website at: **www.navy.com/careers/special-operations/seals.html**.

Conclusion

Becoming a Navy SEAL is without a doubt a rewarding career choice. But as we have seen here, the Navy has high standard as to who can and cannot be accepted into the Navy SEAL program. Did you learn something new about Navy SEALs in this handbook? What was your favorite part? Let's review the main sections.

First, we talked about what a Navy SEAL is. We found out that "SEAL" is actually an acronym that stands for "SEa, Land, and Air". Each SEAL is specially trained to operate in these three areas, and as part of their job they often have to throw themselves out of airplanes! We also learned how long Navy SEALs have been operating in the world- soldiers have been learning unconventional warfare since World War Two! But they were officially formed as "SEALs" in 1961, and they have been especially active since the Vietnam War, where they were called "the men with the green faces".

Then we found out what the training is like to become a Navy SEAL. We saw how all interested recruits must pass through 61 weeks of intense training to receive the SEAL trident. During their training, recruits are pushed to their physical, mental, and emotional limits. What part impressed you the most? Was it the running, the swimming, or the exercises with live ammunition and explosives? Training to be a SEAL is incredibly hard, and only about 10-20% of those who enter the program actually finish it- but for those who make it through the intense training a life of adventure and noble service awaits them!

Then we answered the question: is being a Navy SEAL an easy job? You were able to decide the answer for yourself as you learned about what it's like to be a SEAL and what some past SEAL missions were. Most likely, you would agree with the statement that being a SEAL is really hard. Every day brings new challenges, and each new mission requires 100% from the SEALs who are assigned to it. We looked closely at two recent missions (the rescue of Captain Phillips and the raid on Osama bin Laden's compound) to see how hard the SEALs had to work in order to carry out their mission successfully.

After that, we had an exciting look at an average day for a Navy SEAL. When they are not deployed on a mission, they spend their time constantly training. SEAL missions routinely last from 6-8 months, and they serve in every corner of the world. They train for both cold and hot weather missions, and sometimes they have to spend long days just keeping an eye on their targets.

Then we saw what the hardest part of being a Navy SEAL is. While many people think that the training is the most difficult part, in reality the day to day life of a Navy SEAL can be pretty hard too. Not only do these highly trained soldiers have to be ready to kill other people, but they have to maintain strict secrecy and often go weeks or months without speaking to their family members or visiting them back home.

Then we found out what the future holds for Navy SEALs. In ten years, when you are old enough to become a SEAL, what can you expect the job to be like? We saw that there are new technologies that will make SEALs more effective and even more popular than they are now. More and more, international problems will be resolved by small teams of soldiers carrying out specific objectives, instead of large armies invading each other's borders. Special Forces (like Navy SEALs) will become more useful and necessary in the near future.

Finally, we you learned what steps you can take right now to get ready for an exciting job as a Navy SEAL. Even though you have to be at least 18 to apply for SEAL training, there are several things that you can do now to help with your success. Do you remember the most important thing to do? Educate yourself by talking to current and former SEALs, Navy recruiters, and by doing online research. And, after speaking to your doctor, start a workout program as soon as you can to get the best shape of your life. Only that way will you be able to pass the tests to join the SEAL training program.

Navy SEALs are true heroes. They work in the shadows and do their job without asking for special recognition. 24 hours a day, they are out there carrying out their missions so that

Americans back home can enjoy relative peace and safety. If you are looking for an exciting career, where you can serve with honor and make a difference every day, then perhaps becoming a Navy SEAL is the best option for you!

Navy SEALs dropping onto a destroyer during an exercise[9]

---

[9]   Image   source:
http://commons.wikimedia.org/wiki/File:US_Navy_SEALS_fast_ro
pe.jpg

Made in the USA
San Bernardino, CA
28 August 2014